SCOTLAND'S CENTURY 1900 - 2000

One Hundred Years of Photographs

SCOTLAND'S CENTURY

1900 - 2000

One Hundred Years of
Photographs

168 July 1 1999 HM The Queen formally declares the Scottish Parliament open for business.

167 Raising the standard ! A picture to sum up the hopes and spirit of Scotland at the end of the century. *Ian Rutherford*

165 A disturbing and seemingly omnipresent feature of the 1990s was the appearance of the homeless on the streets of Scotland. This picture was taken at the foot of The Mound, Edinburgh. *Stuart Pennykid*

166 1996 An equally ubiquitous feature of the 1990s was the cellphone. Dismissed as a 'yuppie' toy in the '80s, in the '90s it became a vital personal accessory. Here a mediaeval film extra on the set of *Ivanhoe* gets on the blower. *Hamish Campbell*

162 July 1996 Going down ! A tower at the former British Steel plant at Ravenscraig, Motherwell, is demolished. *Colin McPherson*

163 1994 Challenging authority. The polis stand up to some abuse at an anti-roads demonstration outside New St Andrew's House. *Ian Rutherford*

164 *Opposite* June 1998 Display of national pride. A Scotland supporter celebrates victory over Norway. *Eric McCowat*

160 March 10 1996 Dunblane. Anxious parents, who have just heard of the shooting, dash to Dunblane Primary School. *Allan Milligan*

161 Anniversary of the shootings. Seventeen candles of remembrance lit at Dunblane Cathedral for a memorial service for the 16 children and their teacher who died a year previously. *Chris Bacon*

159 June 1995 The Royal Highland Show at Ingliston provided the photographer with an opportunity for a prizewinning photograph. *Hamish Campbell*

158 April 1994 See you, Jimmy! Duncan Ferguson headbutts John McStay at a Rangers vs Raith Rovers match at Ibrox. Ferguson was later convicted for assault and jailed for three months in October 1995: the first professional footballer in Scotland to go to prison for an offence committed on the pitch. This photograph was eventually used in evidence and the photographer cross-examined in court. *Eric McCowat*

155 March 1993 The Scottish public reacted generously to the disastrous war in Bosnia. Organisations like Edinburgh Direct Aid transported relief to the beleagured and spiritual support was provided by people like Edinburgh composer and musician Professor Nigel Osborne, seen here performing under sniper fire at Sarajevo's ruined Skenderija Stadium. He is playing with Vedran Smailovic, the Sarajevo cellist who symbolised resistance to the Serbian siege, and who eventually escaped Sarajevo with the support of the newspaper *Scotland on Sunday* and came to Scotland. *Paul Harris*

156 *Left* Eighteen year-old Private Andrew Bokas of the 1st Highlanders Regiment, from Lairg in Sutherland, played the pipes in the British war cemetery in Skopje, Macedonia as British troops deployed in support of the international mission in Kosovo in January 1999. *Paul Harris*

157 *Right* October 1994 Peace dividend. A Scottish soldier can now relax with local kids in Belfast. *Ian Rutherford*

153 *Top* January 6 1993 The oil tanker *Braer* aground off the coast of Shetland. This picture shows a mist of oil blowing ashore from the wreck. *Allan Milligan*

154 May 22 1994 Labour leader John Smith's funeral at Iona Abbey. A much respected figure, he failed to live to see his party come to power. *Ian Rutherford*

152 January 1993 Severe flooding hit Tayside. This prizewinning picture was taken in the North Muirton estate, Perth, as a BT engineer tried to phone home.
Ian Rutherford

150   At the races, Musselburgh. *Ian Rutherford*

151   Motorcycle scramble, Hawick, 1994. *Ian Rutherford*

149 1992 Splash ! A horse and rider fall at a water jump at the Scottish Horse trials, Thirlestane Castle. *Ian Rutherford*

147 *Opposite* February 1991 The abbot leads Cisterican monks of Nunraw
Abbey, East Lothian, through the snow on a prayer for peace to end fighting
in the Gulf War. *Douglas Corrance*

148 February 17 1991 First day of redundancy, Ravenscraig. *Douglas Corrance*

Crewmembers of a Polish trawler are rescued by breeches buoy after the ship went aground at Balmedie, near Aberdeen. *Geddes Wood*

145 February 1990 Chicken tonight . . . A cockerel is loosed onto the Murrayfield pitch during the Scotland v France match. *Ian Rutherford*

146 December 10 1990 Raised from the deep. The wreck of the *Antares* surfaces off the Isle of Bute after almost three weeks underwater. *Allan Milligan*

144 This dramatic rugby tackle was captured by a split-second photograph at a game between Edinburgh Select and France at Goldenacre, Edinburgh, in 1987. *Eric Rutherford*

142 *Opposite* July 7 1988 There were two major disasters in 1988. Shortly before 10 p.m. on the night of July 6 a massive explosion and fire engulfed the oil rig Piper Alpha. At the height of the blaze, the flames could be seen 25 miles away. It was the world's worst oilrig disaster and 167 men died despite a major rescue operation. Here it is seen burning the next morning, the derrick lying twisted and collapsed over the remains of the platform. *Hamish Campbell*

143 *Above* December 21 1988 The downed cockpit of Pan Am flight 103, Lockerbie. Around seven in the evening Pan Am flight 103 disappeared from the radar screens at Prestwick Air Traffic Control. The Jumbo jet, with 259 passengers and crew aboard, disintegrated at 31,000 feet as an explosive device was set off. Everyone aboard the aircraft and eleven Lockerbie residents died as the wreckage fell to earth. This picture shows the nose section which landed on Tundergarth Hill. This was the worst disaster in British aviation history and Scotland's greatest disaster of the century. *Ian Rutherford*

141 May 1986 In this intriguing photograph, houses at Methil, Fife, are dwarfed by the Allwyn North oil platform jacket being towed out from the RGC Offshore plant.
Hamish Campbell

139 August 1986 In the shadow of the Forth Rail
Bridge, a disabled swimmer practises for his English
Channel swim. *Douglas Corrance*

140 June 1987 Hawick Common Riding.
Cornet and his followers riding towards
Hawick Moor. *Ian Mackenzie*

137 1986 Old and new Glasgow is graphically captured in this photograph. Hogganfield Street, Blackhill.

138 Riggers on the Forth
Rail Bridge. *Hamish Campbell*

134 August 1985 The Burryman, South Queensferry. In this bizarre annual event a man is coated all over with sticky burrs. *Ian Mackenzie*

135 January 1987 The ancient festival of Burning the Clavie at Burghead, Moray. The Clavie is carried up Doorie Hill. *Ian Mackenzie*

136 Swinging the Balls of Fire to usher in the New Year on the High Street in Stonehaven. *Geddes Wood*

132 May 1984 The infamous police charge at Hunterston power station. A miners' picket is underneath the hooves of the police horses, centre. *Allan Milligan*

133 A striking study of miners' leader Arthur Scargill. *Hamish Campbell*

131 January 1984 A passenger train trapped in the snow at Bridge of Orchy in Perthshire.
Allan Milligan

130 1983 This picture of twenty year-old nurse Shirley Lawson captured the angry mood of nurses when Margaret Thatcher visited Glasgow. The photograph captured the Best News Picture Award and Shirley later became a part-time photographic model. *Ken Ferguson.*

128 June 1 1982 Pure joy as the Pope visits Glasgow. *Charles Donnelly*

129 June 1 1982 The Pope in his specially-built, bulletproof Popemobile arrives at Bellahouston Park, Glasgow, for the public mass. This was the biggest police operation ever held in Scotland.

127 May 31 1982 The Pope's visit to Scotland. In the company of the Moderator of the General Assembly of the Church of Scotland, The Rt Rev Professor John McIntyre, Pope John Paul II passes under the severe gaze of of the statue of John Knox, founder of the Reformation in Scotland.

126 February 1981 'Out of the mouths of babes'. This picture was taken at a right to work rally in Glasgow. The Linwood motor factory - home of the Hillman Imp - faced closure at the time. *Andy Hosie.*

125 1980 Up for Grabs. England 'keeper Ray Clemence makes a flying save against Scotland at Hampden. *Richard Parker*

124 February 1982 The cargo ship *Craigantlet* aground beneath the foghorn
near Portpatrick. *Allan Milligan*

123 June 1980 Southpaw Jim Watt, from Moodiesburn, Glasgow, fights Howard Davis. Watt had become world lightweight champion in April 1979, when he defeated Alfredo Petalua. He defended his title successfully on four occasions until losing it in June 1981 to Alex Arguello.
Allan Milligan

Linda   Norma   Michelle   June   Fiona

120 1979 An unusual picture of a national institution of the time – the so-called Lager Lovelies. The beautiful girls who then adorned Tennent's lager cans for Scottish drinkers pose behind their canned images. *Eric McCowat*

121 *Right* September 1979 Another Lovely of the time . . . Margaret Thatcher in over-shoes at Dounreay nuclear power station. *Allan Milligan*

122 *Opposite* August 1979 Playing in the rain. A picture snapped against the odds. Hibs play Manchester City in the pouring rain in the Skol Tournament at Hearts' ground, Tynecastle. Hibs players pictured are Gordon Rae and Craig Paterson. *Eric McCowat*

118 *Right* 1977 Jock Stein had a reputation for speaking is mind. In this picture he gives a scarf-waving supporter a tongue lashing for running onto the pitch during a game.

119 *Above* 1977 Scotland fans run riot at Wembley, destroying the goalposts, digging up the turf and generally creating mayhem. *Denis Straughan*

116 Patience. This cat seemed to look forward to an early result from the angler. *Hamish Campbell*

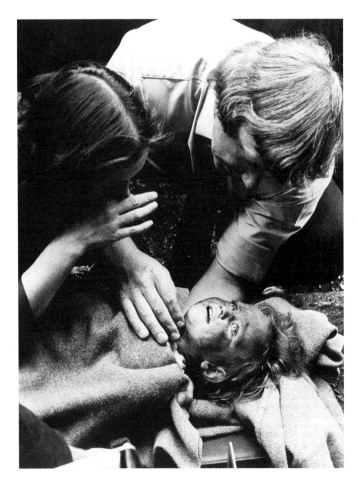

117 August 1975 Dean is Alive ! This youngster, rescued from a burning building in Dundee, at first appeared to be dead. The photograper caught the moment of relief as young Dean suddenly regained consciousness. *RoyCameron*

112 *Top* Out of the rough. Gordon Sherry playing in The Open, St Andrews, 1995. *Hamish Campbell*

113 *Middle* Playing around the obstacle. A golfer at North Berwick seems unflustered by a downed helicopter.

114 *Opposite* Fore letter word? Lee Trevino plays in The Open at Muirfield in 1972. *Stan Hunter*

115 *Left* Harry Bannerman wraps his club around a fence post. *Jack Crombie*

111 At the dog show, Ingliston. *Alan Macdonald*

109 1975 Another industry in decline. A powerful study of a Scottish steelworker as the industry faced a massive unemployment crisis. *William Thornton*

110 Industry on the move in the early 1970s. The first oil from beneath the North Sea aboard the BP oil rig *Sea Quest* is examined by Markinch driller Willie Hunter. *Geddes Wood*

108 1974 HM The Queen got a nudge from police horse Blackie when she opened Edinburgh's new police HQ at Fettes. *Stan Hunter*

107 October 1972 Cheers, Ma'am ! HM The Queen visits Stirling University. This picture scandalised the university. *Hamish Campbell*

106 October 21 1971 The aftermath of the
Clarkston gas explosion. Hundreds of people
were shopping when a huge gas explosion blew
apart the Clarkston shopping complex. Twenty
people were killed and 105 injured as the centre
of the block collapsed like a pack of cards.

104 October 1971 Crunch! A three-wheeler comes to grief. *Hamish Campbell*

105 *Opposite* October 1971 John Brown's shipyard goes into liquidation and Jimmy Reid addresses the work-in at Upper Clyde Shipbuilders. Marathon would take over in April 1972 but the proud era of Clyde shipbuilding was already over.

101 1971 Glasgow's Renfield Street and Detective Inspector George Johnston is slashed by a youth with an open razor. This dramatic picture has been published all over the world. Of course, today, Glasgow Smiles Better . . . *Allan Milligan*

102   November 1971. Bodies are brought down from the mountains. There was tragedy in the Cairngorms as six Edinburgh schoolchildren and their teacher lost their lives in a blizzard in the mountains. Only two survived from the expedition. *Geddes Wood*

103 *Opposite* January 2 1971 The Ibrox disaster. As fans exited down Stairway 13 from the traditional New Year Celtic-Rangers game, Celtic scored in the 89th minute and then Rangers equalised 75 seconds later in injury time. Some fans tried to turn back, others pushed on and within minutes 66 fans were dead - most from suffocation - as the barriers and handrails were bent and twisted by the pressure on the stair.

99 March 1969 Gales lashed Scotland for weeks on end. This dramatic picture was taken of a trawler attempting to reach sanctuary in Aberdeen Harbour. *Geddes Wood*

100 This rather more tranquil scene shows the one time Guinness family's steam yacht, *Ocean Mist*, sailing in the Highlands, Ben Nevis in the background. Two decades later, in 1986, the ship was sailed to Leith where she was moored in the inner harbour as a floating restaurant. *J Pugh*

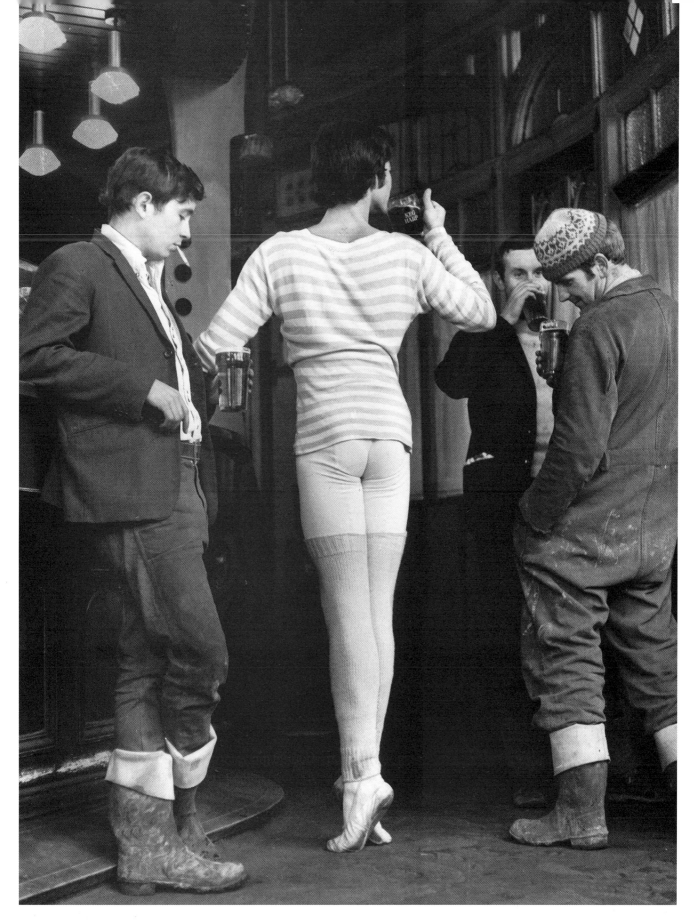

98 1969 Sight for sore eyes ? A puzzling apparition for regulars when ballet dancer Michael Ingleton nipped out from rehearsals for a quick pint in a Glasgow pub. *George McEwan*

94 September 1968 HM The Queen Mother sees off the Balmoral Castle Guard at Glen Muick. The soldiers, from the 1st Battalion The Black Watch, marched all the way back to their barracks at Kirknewton - a distance of over 100 miles. *Geddes Wood*

95 *Below left* November 1968 The James Watt Street fire in Glasgow. Twenty-two workers died behind the barred windows of the upholstery warehouse where they worked.

96 *Below* December 2 1968 This was the only, exclusive, picture of convicted murderess Sheila Garvie leaving Aberdeen Sheriff Court for prison. Together with her lover, Brian Tevendale, she was convicted of murdering her husband, wealthy Mearns farmer Maxwell Garvie, in a trial which scandalised the Aberdeen area with its stories of wife swapping and nudism. *Geddes Wood*

97 1969 Inverness Folk Festival. A remarkable and historic photograph with some 'weel kent', if younger, faces. Back row, left to right: Billy Connolly, Gerry Rafferty, Hamish Henderson, Hamish Bain, Jean Redpath, Archie Fisher, Finbar Furey, Aly Bain, Tam Harvey, Derek Moffat. Front row: Cyril Tawney, Eddie Furey, Tich Frier, Andy Ramage, Ian MacCalman. As Aly Bain put it in June 1999, "What's amazing about this photograph is that we're all still alive!"

90 August 1968 Action man. It took an American to steal the limelight at the Aboyne Highland Games. 'Big Bill' Bangert from Missouri, sporting the MacLeod tartan, putts the shot...

91 Throws the weight...

92 Tosses the caber...

93 and – ultimately – shows what a Scotsman doesn't normally wear beneath the kilt! *Geddes Wood*

88 August 1967 The Missed Penalty.
The faces say it all at this Rangers v.
Dundee United game at Ibrox.
Allan Milligan

89 September 1967 A kilted character
takes a swipe at the Duke of
Edinburgh with his souvenir
programme. This scene at the Braemar
Highland Gathering is not all it seems
– a wasp has settled on the collar of
the Royal personage's jacket!
Geddes Wood

87 September 1967 The QE2 launched from John Brown's shipyard. *Hamish Campbell*

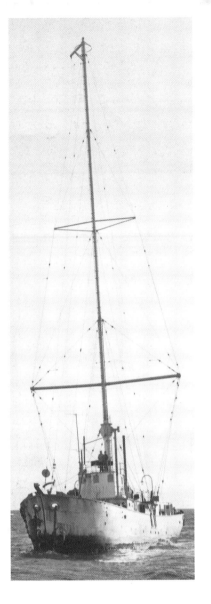

85 *Left* August 15 1967 The pirate radio ship Radio Scotland closed at midnight on August 14 as the Marine Broadcasting Offences Act, outlawing radio ships, came into force.

86 *Below* Here the disc jockeys throw vinyl records overboard from the ship, which was anchored off Dunbar in the Firth of Forth.

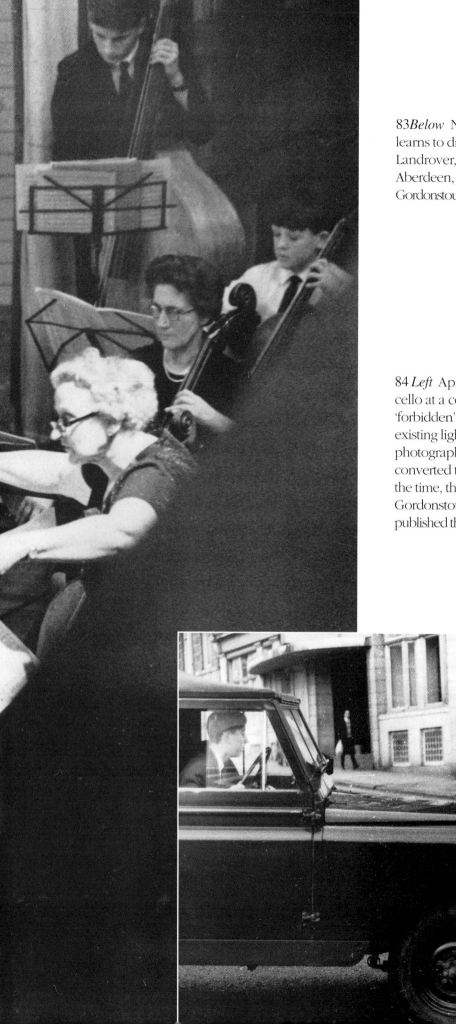

83 *Below* November 1966 Prince Charles learns to drive. At the wheel of his detective's Landrover, he pulls out from the Joint Station, Aberdeen, returning to school at Gordonstoun. *Geddes Wood*

84 *Left* April 1967 Prince Charles plays the cello at a concert in Elgin Town Hall. This 'forbidden' picture was taken using the limited existing light by a Scotpix agency photographer using a pair of opera glasses converted to house an old Leica camera. At the time, the Prince was studying nearby at Gordonstoun School. The picture was widely published throughout the world. *John Palmer*

81 January 1965 The entrance to Aberdeen Harbour is completely blockaded by fishing vessels during the dispute between the Skippers & Mates Association and the owners. *Geddes Wood*

82 *Below* Weighing fish boxes at Oban Pier. *J Pugh*

79 August 1964 Looking
for a bargain. A 'snatch'
picture taken through the
glass of Bell's Antique Shop
in Aberdeen's Bridge Street.
Proprietor Mr W S Bell has
just had a surprise visit from
H M The Queen Mother.
Geddes Wood

80 March 1966 Chasing the
floating voters. Donald Dewar
electioneering in the snow from a
pilot boat in Aberdeen Harbour. He
was subsequently returned to the
Westminster parliament for the first
time for the constituency of
Aberdeen South having ousted the
sitting Conservative member, Lady
Tweedsmuir. At the time he would
never have imagined that thirty-
three years later he would become
first minister in a Scottish
parliament. *Geddes Wood*

78 This Aberdeen snowman dwarfed the home of its young builders! *Geddes Wood*

75 *Above* June 1964 Strict quarantine at Aberdeen's City Hospital in response to the typhoid epidemic. This parent, unable to visit is young son, holds up a message of love. *Geddes Wood*

76 1964 Meet me at Whites ! This used to be the call at the Links Market: the oldest and largest fair to be held in Scotland held each spring on the seafront at Kirkcaldy. *J Pugh*

77 The Round Up – sensation of the age.

72 The Forth Road Bridge starts to take shape in 1959 in the shadow of the old rail bridge. *J Pugh*

73 September 1964 The completed Forth Road Bridge, then the fourth longest suspension bridge in the world, was an engineering marvel of its day, opened by HM The Queen on September 4. *J Pugh*

74 July 1966 The road bridge over the River Tay was opened by HM The Queen Mother on August 18 1966. This view looks towards Dundee from Newport, Dundee Law in the background. At the time, construction cost £8 million. *J Pugh*

68 *Left* 1961 Prime Minister Harold Macmillan plays holiday golf at Nairn. Note the knee patches on his trousers in the days before spin doctors. *Geddes Wood*

69 *Below* July 1961 A young Denis Law trains on Aberdeen beach with local youngsters. *Geddes Wood*

70 *Below* August 1963 This front page picture published in an Aberdeen daily paper was taken by a schoolboy with a camera when a craneman fell into Aberdeen Harbour. *Paul Harris*

71 *Right* January 1963 Prince Charles has a day's skiing in the Cairngorms. This was the day he gave his detective the slip and disappeared in the mountains. *Doug Westland*

66 May 1960 H M Submarine *Narwahl* stranded. When this giant Royal Navy submarine went aground near Campbeltown, the photographer waited until the tide went out. Then he took this photograph in the pitch black of early morning, his camera mounted on a tripod, walking around the stranded vessel firing off his flashgun more than sixty times! *Alex 'Tug' Wilson*

67 1962 This shot of Glasgow Cathedral, down Wishart Street from Alexandria Parade, perfectly captures the icy chill of winter.

65 1960 Just passing through. Elvis Presley, with Mrs Georgina Lehar, at Prestwick Airport en route to national service in Germany. This was the only time The King touched British soil. It is said he looked around and uttered just three immortal words, "Where am I?"

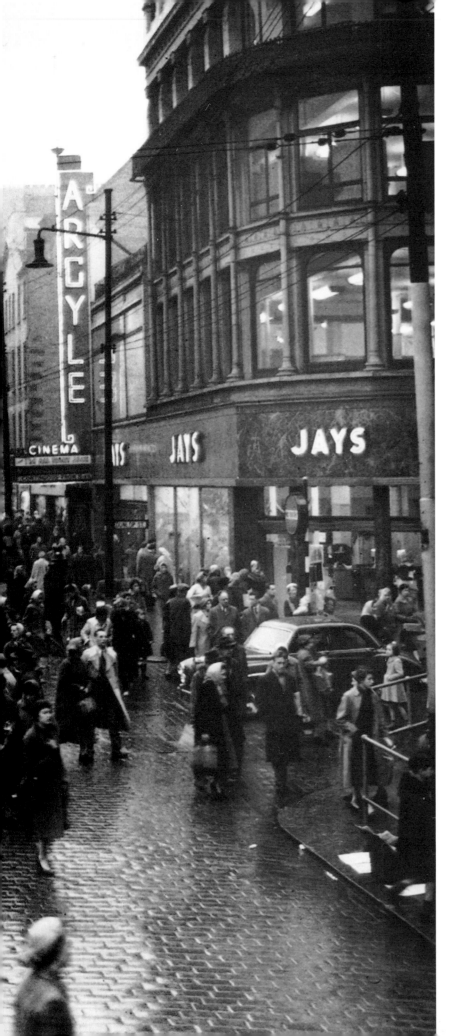

64 1959 A dreich Argyle Street, Glasgow, is thronged with Saturday afternoon shoppers. The trams are still running but cars are few and far between.

63 January 1959 A passing photographer captured this dramatic image of a Glasgow tram ablaze in Old Shettleston Road, Glasgow. A lorry crashed into the tram in thick fog and a 600 volt electricity charge caused by sheared wires set the tram on fire from end to end. Two passengers and the driver died.

60 1957 The legendary Jimmy Shand and his Band.

61 1959 An early picture of actor Sean Connery in his pre-Bond days, appearing in Edinburgh's King's Theatre in *The Seashell*.

62 May 1958 Long before the days of 'political correctness', the Miss UK Contest was held in The Palais, Edinburgh.

58 1954 Roy Rogers and Trigger, his faithful horse, negotiate their way up the main staircase at the Caledonian Hotel in Edinburgh. Only Rogers stayed in the hotel: after the photo opportunity, the horse was sent off to the Scottish Co-op Stables in Edinburgh to bed down with the milk horses. And – even worse – there were actually two Triggers: the stage act was so demanding that one horse could only manage one performance daily. One of the two was ultimately stuffed and thereby immortalised at Roy Rogers' ranch.

59 1956 Eviction for non-payment of rent. During the 1950s this was a feature of life for council house tenants who failed to come up with the rent money.

56 September 29 1952 John Cobb climbs into his speedboat *Crusader* on the shores of Loch Ness. He died later that day in his bid for the world water speed record. *(Inset)* On its last attempt at the record, *Crusader* speeds past Castle Urquhart.

57 September 18 1953 The Grimsby trawler *Hassett* aground at Ackergill, north of Wick, just sixty yards offshore. This aerial shot was taken from a chartered aircraft in the days when newspaper budgets were more elastic than today. Fifteen of the crew of twenty were rescued by breeches buoy. It was reported that the surviving crew members gathered in the bridge and sang 'Land of Hope & Glory'. *Alex 'Tug' Wilson*

55 April 1945 In La Celle, south-east of Paris, soldiers of the 15th Scottish escort German prisoners into captivity on the running board of a commandeered Opel Blitz fire engine. *Sgt. Laing*

52 1942 A rare photograph of the preventive measures taken to exclude German submarines from the Clyde: a boom protects shipping. The picture was taken from above the Cloch Lighthouse looking towards Dunoon. Note the guardships and narrow entry in the middle of the boom. *James Hall*

53 Two captured German airmen are escorted to the police station down Bell Street, Dundee. Their Heinkel was on a bombing mission over the city when it was shot down.

54 *Opposite* May 1941 Bombing of Greenock. Devastation in Cathcart Street.

50 March 1941 Clydebank blitz. The morning after . . .

51 March 17 1941 All that was left of a tram bombed in Nelson Street, Glasgow.

48 May 1941 Young evacuees
leave Glasgow in the wake of
the bombing raids.

49 April 30 1940 Pictured
shortly before she sank in the
River Clyde, the Free French
destroyer *Maille Breze* off
Greenock. *James Hall*

46 February 1940 The luxury liner *Queen Elizabeth*, camouflaged in battleship grey, secretly leaves Clydebank for America. There she would be refitted as a troopship and would carry thousands of GIs across the Atlantic for the ultimate invasion of Europe. With her great turn of speed she successfully criss-crossed the Atlantic without escort, evading predatory U-boats and entered service with Cunard in 1946.

47 1940 Barrage balloons go up on the River Forth to protect the vital Victorian rail bridge. German aircraft made a number of unsuccessful attempts to destroy it but failed.

44 October 28 1939 German Heinkel III bomber downed at Kidlaw near Humbie in East Lothian after an unsuccessful mission over the Forth. Both the Spitfires of City of Glasgow (202) Squadron and City of Edinburgh (603) Squadron claimed the 'kill' although the aircraft was riddled by more than 300 bullets.

45 1943 The technology of war comes to the Hebrides. This dramatic photograph shows a B17 Flying Fortress flying over a traditional croft on Benbecula.

41 1938 The Empire Exhibition by night, Glasgow. *J Pugh*

42 1939 This tranquil view of Glasgow's Botanic Gardens carries no hint of the horrors to be visited on the city in the coming war.

43 1940 The funeral procession of Henry Cullen, Secretary of the Royal & Ancient Golf Club, St. Andrews. In accordance with time honoured tradition, the senior mourners are carrying a black bag full of silver golf balls and a golf club shrouded in black. *George Cowie*

39 1934 Launch of the liner *Queen Mary*.

40 1934 Waulking the
tweed, Eriskay. In the picture,
the new tweed cloth is being
softened by the women, in
traditional Hebridean style,
thumping it with their fists.
W Kissling

37 All dressed up to the nines. Managers of the Union Bank of Scotland and their wives on a night out in Glasgow in 1927, probably to celebrate the opening of their new Head Office.

38 1930 The bank inspectors call . . . These clerks of the Inspector's Department of the Union Bank of Scotland in Glasgow – Misses Robertson, Macdougall, Smith and Laird – don't look a particularly terrifying foursome although doubtless the visit of their department would have been much feared. The photograph was taken on the centenary of the Union Bank.

35 1927 The St Kilda Parliament. The most remote part of Scotland, St Kilda was abandoned on August 30 1930 at the request of the islanders who lived there. Life on what has come to be termed 'the island on the edge of the world', 50 miles west of the Sound of Harris, had simply become unsustainable.

36 September 26 1927 The MacBraynes paddlesteamer *Grenadier* – a regular on the Iona–Staffa run – caught fire during the night at her berth at the North Pier, Oban. The fire was fierce and she sank at her moorings; three of the crew died and she had to be scrapped.

33 1926 An overturned bus is righted in Glasgow during the General Strike.

34 1926 International Workers Relief distribution of food to miners at the lockout, Lochore.

32 1921 This photograph of a newsagent's shop in St Andrews is packed with interest and captures the atmosphere of the early '20s with its array of newspaper posters, advertising and the packed window. And, as it is St Andrews, secondhand golf clubs are for sale from 2s 6d each (i.e. 12.5 new pence) On the steps of his premises at 206 South Street is the proprietor and former professional golfer, Robert B 'Buff' Wilson.

29 June 21 1919 The German High Seas Fleet, interned in the waters of Scapa Flow, is sunk by its officers in what becomes known as 'the Grand Scuttle'. Fifty-two ships went to the bottom. Here the battle cruiser *Derfflinger* sinks beneath the waves.

30 Most of the fleet was salvaged after an engineer called Ernest Cox bought the scuttled fleet from the Admiralty in 1924. Altogether, the firm of Cox & Danks raised 26 destroyers, four battlecruisers, two battleships and a light cruiser. Here the German battleship *Moltke* is seen under tow en route to the Royal Navy dockyard in Rosyth. After a row between pilots, she went adrift and almost destroyed the Forth Rail Bridge.

31 October 10 1920 This dramatic photograph shows the salvage operations ongoing aboard the grounded Aberdeen trawler *Ben Namur* at Bay of Skaill, Orkney. The official enquiry found the vessel went aground in thick fog and a heavy swell after the captain failed to establish his position before setting course. *Thomas Kent*

27 January 31 1919 The Glasgow Strike. With the end of the First World War, the return of soldiers from the front and decline in orders for munitions and war material threatened widespread unemployment. The Clyde Workers' Committee called for a general strike at the end of January and whilst strike leaders were inside the City Chambers strikers were repeatedly charged by riot police. Here the Red Flag is raised in front of the City Chambers in George Square.

28 The army stands by to intervene in the Glasgow Strike. Tanks were parked at the cattle market ready for action against strikers. On February 1 six tanks were rumbling down city centre streets amidst fears of a 'Bolshevist' uprising. The strike soon collapsed as the organisers disagreed about how to carry it forward.

26 1917 An unusual sight in an era of rigid social and class
division. King George V engages a workman at Cammell Laird's
shipyard in conversation.

23 1914 King George V, Queen Mary and Princess Mary visit the children's ward at Perth Royal Infirmary during their tour of Scotland.

24 May 22 1915 The Gretna rail disaster. The worst railway disaster in British history happened when a special troop train, carrying the 7th Royal Scots from their depot at Leith, to Liverpool for embarkation to France, ploughed into a standing local train. The night express from Euston then struck the wreckage. The death toll was 227; the signalmen at Quintinshill were blamed and served terms of imprisonment.

25 May 1915 Funeral of 100 victims of the Gretna rail disaster at Leith. A long line of horsedrawn waggons snaked through Leith taking the victims for burial.

22 1911 Tears won't help . . . . Booked in Edinburgh for stealing 'tumchies' (turnips).

20 1910 Dancing to the brass band, St Andrews during Lammas Market. The location is at the side of the town kirk.

21 1910 Dutch style costumes at Lammas Market, St Andrews, draw attention to the historic links with the Low Countries.

19 1905 Laying granite setts between the tramlines at the foot of Leith Walk, Leith.

17 July 1906 Inchgreen rail accident. On the line from Princes Pier, Greenock, to Overton paper Mill in Ayrshire, a runaway train jumped the embankment at the foot of a hill and landed in a field.

18 August 9 1907. The barquentine *Celtic* was wrecked near Sandwick, Orkney. She was damaged by a storm at sea and – her fore topmast broken – drifted ashore. *H Robertson*

13 1904 The classic steam yacht *Medea* was built on the Clyde at the yard of Alexander Stephen & Son for William Macalister Hall, laird of of Torrisdale Castle on Kintyre, and launched on August 29 1904. She took just 51 days to build and was amongst the finest of her type. Symptomatic of an age of opulence when many private steam yachts were built on the Clyde, she was used for shooting cruises as well as for normal transport purposes at a time when road communications were poor. Elegantly fitted out and with decks of teak, the 110 foot long yacht cost £6,750.

14 The after smoking cabin was panelled in oak.

15 Today, she survives preserved as an exhibit at the San Diego Maritime Museum.

16 The magnificent dragon prow of the steam yacht *Sapphire*, built by John Brown's for the Duke of Bedford and launched 1912.

12 May 13 1903 The visit of King Edward and Queen Alexandra to Edinburgh. Princes Street was extravagantly decorated for the occasion.

10 1902 A dancing bear in the centre of Dumfries.

11 1908 A street ventriloquist in the Grassmarket, Edinburgh.

7 Around the turn of the century rural life had little changed since the earliest times. Modern technology was yet to make any impact on agricultural communities. Carrying freshly cut peats on Lewis. *Dr I F Grant*

8 Around 1900. Packing St Kilda cloth. *R C MacLeod of MacLeod*

9 Ploughing at Poolewe. *Dr I F Grant*

4 'Doon the Watter' at the turn of the century. The paddle steamer *Benmore* leaves the Broomielaw in Glasgow for Kilmun, Dunoon, Rothesay and the Kyles of Bute. *George Washington Wilson*

5 *Below left* Around 1900 Raspberry pickers at Essendy, near Blairgowrie. In the early part of the century more than 80% of the soft fruit picked in Britain came from this part of Tayside. Traditionally, fruit picking in the summer provided a 'holiday' in the fresh air for many workers from Dundee. *Davidson*

6 *Below* On the road. The intriguingly named Swindle Death & Co: a theatre company which toured rural Scotland in Edwardian times.

3 'Caught on the Hop'. This turn of the century image unusually captures the *joie de vivre* of a spot of dancing in the open air in the northeast of Scotland. Most photographs of the time were heavily posed, static creations. *George Washington Wilson*

forbidden Second World War images which never ever appeared in the public print for security reasons (46, 49, 52). So much for *my* favourites . . .

As the 20th century dawned, although Scotland had a quite remarkable track record for invention and innovation in photography, the techniques available then would hardly be recognised today. The cumbersome glass plate camera ruled unchallenged despite all its limitations of time, exposure and number of frames which might be captured. Photography was strictly for the professional and usually required a visit to the studio where likenesses were painstakingly prepared and processed. What we have come to know as 'candid' photography – unposed shots *au naturel* – were virtually unknown which is why some of the earlier images reproduced in this book are so interesting.

Reproduction techniques for newspapers and magazines were still primitive by any standard we can understand today, and actually getting images onto the printed page took time, patience and investment. Although cameras gradually became smaller and, around the middle of the century, the vastly more convenient 35mm. film started to replace the glass plate, there was still much in the way of artifice associated with photography.

By the end of the century, the story was very different. During the 1990s ever smaller chips meant digital technology could – where it was either necessary or desirable – eliminate conventional film and the regime of the darkroom. Professional digital cameras introduced a new era in which an image could be taken, downloaded onto a laptop computer and sent back to the picture desk of a newspaper – courtesy of a cellphone or satellite telephone – in a matter of seconds.

Today everyone is a photographer. The technology is cheap and it is available. Theoretically, at least, anybody can take a great photograph. In practice, very few of us ever do. All the benefits of modern technological wizardry have somehow failed to make us all into great photographers. There are flukes, of course, but, as the old adage goes, it's the man or woman behind the camera who makes the picture, not the camera itself.

May it ever be thus.

INTRODUCTION

The archives of the newspapers, libraries, museums and businesses in Scotland which were searched for this book probably contain – at a rough estimate – around fifty million photographs. This book contains 170 which raises the question: How do you distil down to 170 from fifty million?

Of course, just to look at fifty million photographs could form the basis of a life's work, without actually getting started on putting a book together. So the search inevitably has to start with certain preconceived requirements. The photographs here seek to cover the widest possible geographical spread: from St Kilda in the north-west to Dumfries in the south, from Eriskay to East Lothian. They also seek to embrace a wide range of activity showing Scots at work and at leisure: shipbuilders, miners, farmers, raspberry pickers, bankers, actors and criminals; golfers, footballers, rugby players and sports fans. Then there are two World Wars and some of the most dramatic news events of the century: Lockerbie, Dunblane, Piper Alpha, the Braer disaster, the Gretna rail disaster and the opening of Scotland's very own parliament in July of 1999. From the great and the good, from Pope to royalty, to the poor and the downtrodden, from strikers to the homeless. All are represented here to some degree. Wherever possible, the search has been for the best image. Somebody once said, "A picture can be worth 1,000 words." Equally, it can often be said that the best picture doesn't even need a caption; the image says it all, is self-explanatory. The images here are certainly amongst the best available – if not the actual best – but, ultimately, the choice is subjective.

Some of the images here must , however, be icons for their time; images implanted on all our consciousness, albeit subliminally: the raising of the Scottish Standard on Arthur's Seat, with all its implied recollection of the US Pacific victory on Iwo Jima (167); the downed cocpkit of Pan Am flight 103 on Tundergarth Hill (143); the BT engineer, up to his armpits in water, phoning home, or wherever (152); Scotland fans destroying the Wembley goalposts (119); the broken stairway in the wake of the Ibrox disaster (103); Jimmy Reid exhorting the workers at Upper Clyde Shipbuilders (105); and striking workers raising the Red Flag in front of Glasgow City Chambers (27).

Then there are images which are fascinating for quite the opposite reason: pictures little seen, published maybe just once in a daily paper and, in the nature of the newspaper business, wrapping fish and chips by the next: Donald Dewar electioneering before he ever became an MP (80); Scots soldiers taking German soldiers into captivity on the running board of a fire engine (55); and those

COPYRIGHT HOLDERS

Photographers, where known, are acknowledged alongside their photographs. All photographs are copyright the undernoted

1 Scotpix, Aberdeen
2 The Scotsman Publications Ltd
3 Aberdeen City Library Reference & Local Studies Dept.
4 Aberdeen University Library George Washington Wilson Collection
5 A K Bell Library, Perth & Kinross Council Davidson Collection
6 The Scottish Life Archive National Museums of Scotland
7 Edinburgh City Libraries, Dr I F Grant Collection
8 The School of Scottish Studies, University of Edinburgh
9 Edinburgh City Libraries, Dr I F Grant Collection
10 The Ewart Library, Dumfries & Galloway Library, Information & Archives Dept.
11 Edinburgh City Libraries
12 Edinburgh City Libraries
13 Paul Harris Collection
14 Paul Harris Collection
15 Paul Harris Collection
16 By kind permission of the Keeper of Records of Scotland
17 Paul Harris Collection
18 Paul Harris Collection
19 Edinburgh City Libraries
20 The St Andrews Preservation Trust Museum
21 The St Andrews Preservation Trust Museum
22 Edinburgh City Libraries
23 The Press Association, London
24 Paul Harris Collection
25 Paul Harris Collection
26 The Press Association
27 The Herald & Evening Times
28 The Herald & Evening Times
29 Paul Harris Collection
30 Paul Harris Collection
31 Paul Harris Collection
32 St Andrews Preservation Trust Museum
33 The Herald & Evening Times
34 The Gallacher Memorial Library, Glasgow Caledonian University Library
35 The School of Scottish Studies, University of Edinburgh
36 Moir & Crawford Collection
37 The Governor & Company of the Bank of Scotland
38 The Governor & Company of the Bank of Scotland
39 The Scotsman Publications Ltd
40 The School of Scottish Studies, University of Edinburgh
41 Paul Harris Collection
42 The Herald & Evening Times
43 The St Andrews Preservation Trust Museum
44 Paul Harris Collection
45 Mr Mike Hughes
46 By kind permission of the Keeper of the Records of Scotland
47 The Scotsman Publications Ltd
48 The Herald & Evening Times
49 Norman Burniston
50 The Herald & Evening Times
51 The Herald & Evening Times
52 Norman Burniston
53 Dundee Courier, D C Thomson & Co Ltd
54 The Glasgow Bulletin
55 Imperial War Museum, London
56 The Scotsman Publications Ltd
57 Alex Wilson
58 The Scotsman Publications Ltd
59 The Scotsman Publications Ltd
60 The Scotsman Publications Ltd
61 The Scotsman Publications Ltd
62 The Scotsman Publications Ltd
63 The Scottish Daily Record & Sunday Mail, Glasgow
64 The Herald & Evening Times
65 The Scottish Daily Record & Sunday Mail, Glasgow
66 Alex Wilson
67 The Herald & Evening Times
68 Scotpix, Aberdeen
69 Scotpix, Aberdeen
70 Paul Harris Collection
71 Scotpix, Aberdeen
72 Paul Harris Collection
73 Paul Harris Collection
74 Paul Harris Collection
75 Scotpix, Aberdeen
76 Paul Harris Collection
77 Paul Harris Collection
78 Scotpix, Aberdeen
79 Scotpix, Aberdeen
80 Scotpix, Aberdeen
81 Scotpix, Aberdeen
82 Paul Harris Collection
83 Scotpix, Aberdeen
84 Scotpix, Aberdeen
85 Paul Harris Collection
86 Paul Harris Collection
87 The Scotsman Publications Ltd
88 The Scotsman Publications Ltd
89 Scotpix, Aberdeen
90 Scotpix, Aberdeen
91 Scotpix, Aberdeen
92 Scotpix, Aberdeen
93 Scotpix, Aberdeen
94 Scotpix, Aberdeen
95 The Scottish Daily Record & Sunday Mail
96 Scotpix, Aberdeen
97 The School of Scottish Studies, University of Edinburgh
98 The Scottish Daily Record & Sunday Mail
99 Scotpix, Aberdeen
100 Paul Harris Collection
101 The Scotsman Publications Ltd
102 Scotpix, Aberdeen
103 The Scottish Daily Record & Sunday Mail
104 The Scotsman Publications Ltd
105 The Scotsman Publications Ltd
106 The Scottish Daily Record & Sunday Mail
107 The Scotsman Publications Ltd
108 Stanley Hunter
109 The Scottish Daily Record & Sunday Mail
110 Scotpix, Aberdeen
111 The Scotsman Publications Ltd
112 The Scotsman Publications Ltd
113 The Scotsman Publications Ltd
114 Stanley Hunter
115 The Scotsman Publications Ltd
116 The Scotsman Publications Ltd
117 The Scottish Daily Record & Sunday Mail
118 The Scottish Daily Record & Sunday Mail
119 The Scotsman Publications Ltd
120 The Scottish Daily Express
121 The Scotsman Publications Ltd
122 Eric McCowat
123 The Scotsman Publications Ltd
124 The Scotsman Publications Ltd
125 The Scottish Daily Record & Sunday Mail
126 The Scottish Daily Record & Sunday Mail
127 The Press Association
128 The Scottish Daily Record & Sunday Mail
129 The Press Association
130 The Scottish Daily Record & Sunday Mail
131 The Scotsman Publications Ltd
132 The Scotsman Publications Ltd
133 The Scotsman Publications Ltd
134 Ian Mackenzie, The School of Scottish Studies
135 Ian Mackenzie, The School of Scottish Studies
136 Scotpix, Aberdeen
137 The Herald & Evening Times
138 The Scotsman Publications Ltd
139 Douglas Corrance
140 Ian Mackenzie, School of Scottish Studies
141 The Scotsman Publications Ltd
142 The Scotsman Publications Ltd
143 The Scotsman Publications Ltd
144 The Scottish Daily Record & Sunday Mail
145 The Scotsman Publications Ltd
146 The Scotsman Publications Ltd
147 Douglas Corrance
148 Douglas Corrance
149 The Scotsman Publications Ltd
150 The Scotsman Publications Ltd
151 The Scotsman Publications Ltd
152 The Scotsman Publications Ltd
153 The Scotsman Publications Ltd
154 The Scotsman Publications Ltd
155 Paul Harris Collection
156 Paul Harris Collection
157 The Scotsman Publications Ltd
158 The Scottish Daily Express
159 The Scotsman Publications Ltd
160 The Scotsman Publications Ltd
161 The Press Association
162 Colin McPherson
163 The Scotsman Publications Ltd
164 The Scottish Daily Express
165 Stuart Pennykid
166 The Scotsman Publications Ltd
167 The Scotsman Publications Ltd
168 The Scotsman Publications Ltd

ACKNOWLEDGEMENTS

My thanks go to Bill Brady of *The Scotsman*, Edinburgh; J Geddes Wood of Scotpix, Aberdeen; and Pat Baird and Colin Macmillan of *The Scottish Daily Record & Sunday Mail*, Glasgow, all of whom allowed free and unfettered access to their extensive collections. Special thanks go to Bill Brady and Geddes Wood who also offered much in the way of time, advice and contacts.

Thank you also to other press sources which were drawn upon: Ian Watson, Information Services Manager, *The Herald & Evening Times*; Lorna Machray, The Press Association, London; Express Newspapers, Glasgow; and the D C Thomson Syndication Department, Dundee.

Various individuals and businesses opened up their private collections and I am grateful to Mr Mike Hughes; Peter Moir of Moir Crawford; to Seonaid McDonald of the Archives Department at the Bank of Scotland and The Governor and Company of the Bank of Scotland.

My thanks go to the various public collections which cooperated in supply of many of the more historic images: the A K Bell Library, Perth & Kinross Council (Davidson Collection); The St Andrews Preservation Trust Museum; The Ewart Library and Dumfries & Galloway Library, Information & Archives Department; Edinburgh City Libraries; Aberdeen City Library - Reference & Local Studies Department; Aberdeen University Library, George Washington Wilson Collection; Gallacher Memorial Library, Glasgow Caledonian University Library; The School of Scottish Studies, University of Edinburgh; the Scottish Life Archive, National Museums of Scotland; and The Imperial War Museum, London.

Finally, thanks to those individual photographers who scoured their files and came up with pictures: Ian F Mackenzie; Eric McCowat, Stan Hunter, Colin McPherson, Douglas Corrance and Stewart Pennykid; and Allan Milligan for looking back through his notebooks.

Paul Harris
July 1999

First published 1999 by

Lomond Books
36 West Shore Road
Granton
Edinburgh EH5 1QD

ISBN 0 947782 19 2

A Paul Harris book for Lomond Books

Paul Harris Editorial & Publishing Services
Whittingehame House
Haddington EH41 4QA
journoharris@compuserve.com

Research Susan Nickalls
Design & layout Eddie Clark
Photographs scanned by Syntax, Edinburgh
Printed in the Republic of Slovenia
by Gorenjski Tisk Printing Co.

Previous pages

1 The man behind the camera is Lord Hailsham at an
Aberdeen shipyard launch in July 1962. *Geddes Wood*,
Scotpix, Aberdeen
2 A World War II Spitfire over the Forth Rail Bridge,
June 1993. *Ian Rutherford*, The Scotsman Publications Ltd

Front cover
'Raising the Standard' by Ian Rutherford, The Scotsman
Publications Ltd
Back cover
'Soldier with cellphone' by Hamish Campbell,
The Scotsman Publications Ltd.

Paul Harris

PS853

Lomond Books